BIBLE BAPTISM

CHAPTER 1.

BAPTISM WITH WATER— ITS IMPORTANCE AND MEANING

There have been too many sermons on baptism as a part of the doctrines of some denomination. There is too much talk about "Baptist doctrine" or "Methodist doctrine" or "the doctrine of our church." In this Bible study, we are interested solely in what the Bible teaches about baptism. Nothing else matters. God's people should be baptized because God commanded it, not because some church requires it. They should be baptized a certain way, because that is the way the Bible teaches, and it should have a certain meaning, the meaning which God gave to baptism. People need to remember what the Lord says about baptism, and then do what He says, because He said so.

BAPTISM IN THE BIBLE ALWAYS MEANS WITH WATER, UNLESS OTHERWISE STATED

We use the term **baptism,** not **water baptism,** since that is the way it is used in the Bible. The word **baptism** used in the Bible always means baptism with water, unless otherwise plainly indicated in that particular passage. There is a baptism of the Holy Ghost, but everywhere it is mentioned in the Bible it is plainly called that. The term **baptism,** used without a plain mention of the Holy Spirit, in the Bible, never means baptism of the Holy Spirit. But the term **baptism** without the mention of water, in the Bible, nearly always means baptism with water. Of the verses in the Bible which specially mention **baptism, baptizing, baptized,** etc., there are sixty-nine verses which refer to baptism in water, but only eight say baptism with water. In those eight cases, the term **water** is used because in each case the baptism of the Holy Spirit is also mentioned in the same passage. The simple word **baptism,** in the Bible, refers to baptism with water, unless clearly indicated otherwise.

Remember that Christian baptism was instituted by John the Baptist, and that under his ministry and that of Jesus and His disciples, thousands of people had been baptized in the three or four years before the disciples were baptized with the Holy Ghost at Pentecost. The term **baptism** had a clearly recognized meaning referring to baptism in water long before that time. We may say that literal baptism is with water, but the term is used symbolically about the Holy Spirit, or about the sufferings of Christ, or the burial of Israel under the cloud, surrounded by the Red Sea.

The coming of the Holy Spirit upon a Christian is sometimes called a "baptism," sometimes a "filling," sometimes an "anointing," and sometimes "the gift of the Holy Ghost." On the other hand, the ceremony of Christian baptism in water has no other name in the Bible. The primary and literal meaning of the word **baptism** in the Bible is water baptism. When the word **baptism** is used in the Bible, always take it to refer to water baptism unless that passage of the Scripture plainly shows that the Lord speaks of something else.

For instance, in Ephesians 4:5, "One Lord, one faith, one baptism," the Lord clearly refers to water baptism as He does everywhere else in the New Testament when the simple term is used without explanation or modification. It is a very foolish mistake, then, to use that verse as an excuse for leaving off water baptism when Jesus Himself submitted to it as an act of righteousness which He said is becoming for us to fulfill. Jesus commanded His disciples to baptize the converts among "all nations" and the preachers in New Testament times followed that plain command, whether with Jews or Gentiles, everywhere they went. Ephesians 4:5 simply says that there is only one Lord, one kind of faith, and one kind of water baptism. So in this study when we say **baptism,** we mean what the Lord meant by **baptism,** that is, the burial of the believer in water, as the first ceremony of his Christian life.

THE IMPORTANCE OF BAPTISM

There have been two great errors in regard to baptism. Some people teach that one cannot be saved without baptism. That is a great mistake as we will show. But another very great error is to teach that baptism is a matter of no importance and that we should not insist upon any particular manner or teaching about baptism. How foolish that is, you will see.

There are only two ceremonies which Jesus ever gave for every New Testament Christian to observe: baptism and the Lord's Supper. Of these, baptism was given first and is mentioned about ten times as often in the New Testament as is the Lord's Supper. In the ministry of John the Baptist it is repeatedly mentioned that multitudes were baptized. When Jesus began His ministry, the large number baptized by His direction overshadowed even the baptizing of the converts by John the Baptist, as you see from John 3:22-26 and John 4:1, 2.

It is especially mentioned of the converts at Pentecost in Acts 2:41 that

> **"Then they that gladly received his word were baptized: and the same day there were added unto them about three thousand souls."**

Concerning Philip's great revival in Samaria, we are told in Acts 8:12

> **"But when they believed Philip preaching the things concerning the kingdom of God, and the name of Jesus Christ, they were baptized, both men and women."**

The book of Acts especially mentions again and again that the converts were baptized, as:

The Ethiopian eunuch in Acts 8:38,
Paul, the apostle, Acts 9:18,
Cornelius and his household, Acts 10:47-48.
Lydia, the quiet convert, Acts 16:15,
The Philippian jailer, Acts 16:33, and
Crispus, the chief ruler of the synagogue, Acts 18:8.

Paul even baptized again some converts who had believed on Christ and had been baptized by Apollos, simply because they had missed some of the joyful meaning and blessing of the Holy Spirit in connection with their first baptism (Acts 19:1-7). The New Testament puts baptism in the limelight everywhere people were saved.

BAPTISM PLAINLY COMMANDED

The Lord Jesus commanded baptism, and nothing is unimportant when Jesus commanded it. Jesus Himself chose to be baptized, and that publicly (Matthew 3:13-17). God the Father was pleased with it and spoke aloud from Heaven saying, "This is my beloved Son, in whom I am well pleased." The Holy Spirit came in visible form like a dove to rest on Jesus, so that all could see that the filling of the Holy Spirit comes from obeying the Father, as Jesus obeyed Him then.

There are only three commands in the Great Commission, and baptism is one of them. Jesus reminded the disciples of His authority and then said in Matthew 28:19, 20:

> **"Go ye therefore, and teach all nations, baptizing them in the name of the Father, and of the Son, and of the Holy Ghost: Teaching them to observe all things whatsoever I have commanded you: and, lo, I am with you alway, even unto the end of the world. Amen."**

The apostles were to get people saved, baptize them, and teach them to observe all things Jesus commanded. The only thing that should come before baptism is salvation. Everything else should follow it. Unfortunately baptism is a matter of controversy, and so preachers do not usually give it the prominence which Jesus commanded, and which New Testament preachers gave it, but we ought to. The Bible makes baptism important.

The Great Commission, commanding baptism, applies to "all nations" (Matt. 28:19); to "all the world" and more than that, "to every creature," who hears the gospel and believes in Christ (Mark 16:15). Wherever men hear the gospel and believe, there they ought to be baptized, whether Jew or Gentile, black or white, old or young, in Bible times or now.

NEW TESTAMENT PREACHERS BAPTIZED AS JESUS COMMANDED

Apostles and preachers in the New Testament followed this command of Jesus. In their first great revival, at Pentecost, when men asked, "What shall we do?" Peter told them to "repent and be baptized." Peter did not mean that salvation depended on baptism: they were to repent and then be baptized to declare and confess the remission of their sins. He was simply putting stress, where Jesus placed it, on immediately following Christ in baptism after conversion. We are led to believe from Acts 2:41 that three thousand of the converts were baptized the day of Pentecost. Philip taught the eunuch to be baptized, and as soon as he was convinced that the eunuch believed with all his heart, according to Acts 8:38,

> **"He commanded the chariot to stand still: and they went down both into the water, both Philip and the eunuch; and he baptized him."**

Peter, with the authority of an apostle, "commanded" Cornelius and his household "to be baptized in the name of the Lord" (Acts 10:48). In fact, New Testament preachers took the command of Jesus about baptizing converts so literally that they almost invariably baptized the converts the same day they professed faith in Christ, often the same hour. Paul and Silas baptized the Philippian jailer and his family "the same hour of the night," even though it was past midnight when they were converted! Our modern custom of waiting until once a year, or at best until the close of a revival meeting to baptize people, is unscriptural and must displease the Saviour. People ought to be baptized as soon as possible after they are converted. Baptism is important.

THE MEANING OF BAPTISM

It becomes apparent in reading the New Testament, especially the book of Acts, that baptism was a public and open profession of faith in Christ as Saviour. There is not a single Bible instance where any one was baptized without claiming to have a change of heart. Sometimes the word repentance is used, sometimes belief, etc., referring to the same penitent turning of a heart to Christ in saving faith, as coming before baptism. But in no case recorded in the Scriptures was one baptized who did not already claim salvation. John the Baptist demanded evidence of repentance before he would baptize the Pharisees and Sadduces who came to him (Matt. 3: 7-8). Philip would not baptize the eunuch until he was convinced that he believed in Christ, even "with all thine heart," according to Acts 8:37. In the Great Commission, in Acts 2:38, and everywhere else, repentance and faith in Christ are put ahead of baptism.

BAPTISM A PUBLIC PROFESSION OF FAITH

New Testament Christians understood that when they were baptized, they were publicly putting on Christ before the world. Paul said to the Galatians, "For as many of you as have been baptized into Christ have put on Christ" (Gal. 3:27). Concerning the meaning of baptism, Paul said in Romans 6:3-5:

> **"Know ye not, that so many of us as were baptized into Jesus Christ were baptized into his death? Therefore we are buried with him by baptism into death: that like as Christ was raised up from the dead by the glory of the Father, even so we also should walk in newness of life. For if we have been planted together in the likeness of his death, we shall be also in the likeness of his resurrection."**

The new convert goes down into a watery grave, picturing the burial of Christ and picturing his own death to sin, the crucifixion of the natural man. When he rises, he should know that as he was "planted in the likeness" of the death of Christ, he should also be "in the likeness of His resurrection." At baptism, then, one professes that he believes in that old, old story that Christ died for our sins, was buried, and rose again! He professes that he has had a change in his heart, that he now belongs to Christ, that he means henceforth to live for Christ.

CHAPTER II.

BAPTISM IS CHRISTIAN, NOT JEWISH; NEW TESTAMENT, NOT OLD TESTAMENT; GRACE, NOT LAW

Down through the centuries till modern times all Bible students and theologians agreed that baptism was a New Testament practice exclusively, that it went with the gospel of salvation through faith in Christ, and was not a part of the Old Testament ceremonial law. However, those who sprinkled unconverted babies tried to find some excuse for family baptizings, and so sought to show a similarity, at least, between circumcision and baptism as an argument for the sprinkling of babies which they got from Rome. That was the first time anyone used Old Testament texts as if they applied to baptism, or in any way connected baptism with the Old Testament.

Then in recent years a new cult of ultradispensationalists appeared taking up that argument and expanding it as an excuse for omitting baptism and breaking the command of Christ that converts were to be baptized "even unto the end of the world." Such faddists say that baptism was simply ceremonial law, that John the Baptist was preaching and baptizing on legal ground, that that was in a Jewish dispensation, like circumcision, that now Christians should not be baptized. That is simply one of the false isms of these last days, of which Christians should beware.

BAPTISM NOT LIKE CIRCUMCISION

However, the Bible is as plain as daylight on this matter. Baptism is never mentioned as connected with ceremonial law or as applying to Jews any more than to others. In fact, baptism is not even mentioned in the Old Testament. Any man who puts baptism on a basis with circumcision surely never studied the matter with an unbiased mind. Circumcision was given to Abraham in the book of Genesis, (Gen. 17:9-14), separating him and his descendants from the rest of the race. It was incorporated in the Mosaic law for Israel only, (Lev. 12:3). In the New Testament then we are plainly told that Gentile Christians are not subject to this law, (Acts 15:1-20, Gal. 5:2, 6, and Gal. 6:15.) On the contrary, baptism was not in the Mosaic law, not commanded to Jews as a race anywhere, but commanded to Christians, whether Jews or Gentiles, after conversion. Baptism began with John the Baptist, and as given in the Great Commission in Matthew 28:18-20, goes on to "the end of the world" or the end of this church age. Baptism began when circumcision ended. The Bible plainly tells when baptism began and when circumcision ended. The Bible plainly tells that circumcision now avails nothing and is not to be required of converts. The Bible says nothing like that about baptism. If the Lord had planned for baptism to stop, He would have plainly said so, but He did not say so. Christians who take the Bible, then, cannot throw away baptism.

THE GOSPEL OF JOHN THE BAPTIST EXACTLY THE SAME AS THAT OF CHRIST AND APOSTLES

Laboring to find an excuse for omitting baptism and doing away with this blessed reminder of Christ's death and burial, some people insist that John the Baptist preached a different gospel than Christ and Paul preached, and that Jews were baptized by John the Baptist because they were saved in a different way. How wrong that is! It grows out of a lack of understanding of the Bible doctrine on salvation throughout the Bible. One good man was first a Roman Catholic and believed that people were saved by baptism, and then a Presbyterian and believed that little babies were put under covenant by baptism and that baptism took the place of circumcision, and then joined the Disciples of Christ, a group who teach that people are saved only in baptism, and who often hold that the baptism must be performed by one of their own members or it is not effective. Now he is an ultra-dispensationalist; and out of that muddled background, with no sound theological training, and no broad understanding of the Bible, he teaches that baptism is now done away with entirely, that John the Baptist baptized Jews because they could not be saved without baptism, but that now an added revelation has come of "church truth," that John's baptism was only a part of the Law, that it was for Jews only, that it was once essential to salvation, and is now out of date! That sounds too silly to deserve attention, but some good people who do not know their Bibles and have not been well founded in the great doctrines of salvation, have been misled by it.

The simple truth is that there has never been but one kind of salvation. Peter said, in preaching to Cornelius in Acts 10:43, that "To him (Christ) give all the prophets witness, that through his name whosoever believeth in him shall receive remission of sins." Wait! Read that again! Every prophet in the Old Testament, as well as New Testament apostles, agree, says this Scripture, that all who trust in Christ are instantly saved! Animal sacrifices, baptism, the Lord's Supper, good deeds, never were essential to salvation. Salvation is by faith in Christ alone. It always was the same.

But the doctrine of John the Baptist was exactly the same as that of Christ Himself and of the apostles. It is true that John the Baptist preached, "Repent ye: for the kingdom of heaven is at hand" (Matt. 3:2). He refused to baptize the Pharisees and Sadducees without evidence of repentance. But Jesus preached exactly the same thing, "Repent: for the kingdom of heaven is at hand" (Matt. 4:17). And even when Jews were rejecting their King, and when the kingdom offered was no longer imminent, that is, at hand, still Jesus continued to preach the same doctrine, "Repent!" In Luke 13:1-5 we are told:

> **"There were present at that season some that told him of the Galilaeans, whose blood Pilate had mingled with their sacrifices. And Jesus answering said unto them, Suppose ye that these Galilaeans were sinners above all the Galilaeans, because they suffered such things? I tell you, Nay: but, except ye repent, ye shall all likewise perish. Or those eighteen, upon whom the tower in Siloam fell, and slew them, think ye that they were sinners above all men that dwelt in Jerusalem?**

I tell you, Nay: but, except ye repent, ye shall all likewise perish."

Repentance was Christ's plan of salvation. And when He gave the disciples the Great Commission, as reported in Luke, He said unto them, "That repentance and remission of sins should be preached in his name among all nations, beginning at Jerusalem" (Luke 24:47). It was just another way of stating His plan of salvation "among all nations." All who honestly repent—that is all who turn, in the heart, from sin to God—certainly trust in Christ. So repentance and faith are inseparable.

And Paul preached the same thing, namely that God "commandeth all men every where to repent" (Acts 17:30). It is silly, then, to say that repentance is only for Jews. Actually, repentance means a change of mind, a heart's turning from sin toward God. And of course every person who was ever saved in the Old Testament or the New turned his heart from sin toward God, that is, he repented, as he trusted.

It is true that the Gospel of John stresses faith, trusting in Christ for salvation, but so too did John the Baptist! We are accustomed to quoting John 3:16 and John 3:18, saying that one who trusted in Christ should never perish but have everlasting life and is not condemned. But often people forget that in the same chapter, from verse 27 on, John the Baptist is talking, and he says in John 3:36, "He that believeth on the Son hath everlasting life: and he that believeth not the Son shall not see life; but the wrath of God abideth on him." So then John the Baptist taught that the only way to be saved was by faith in Christ, personal dependence and trust in Him. Repentance and faith are simply different ways of referring to the heart's turning to God, the surrender to and trust in Christ as Saviour. John the Baptist preached exactly the same gospel as did Christ and as did Peter and as did Paul, and exactly the same gospel as we must preach today.

When John the Baptist said, in Matthew 3:11, "I indeed baptize you with water unto repentance," the word **unto** is a translation of the Greek word **eis**, a preposition of reference, and actually John the Baptist simply meant that he baptized people with reference to or in remembrance of, or pointing to, their repentance. He expressly refused to baptize anybody **until they had already repented**, that is, had already turned to Christ, trusting Him and being saved (Matt. 3:7-8). The gospel preached by John the Baptist was exactly the same gospel as preached by the Saviour and by the apostles and taught throughout the New Testament. To say that John the Baptist was in a different dispensation, or that baptism, as administered by John, had a different meaning from that which baptism has today, shows a lack of understanding of the doctrine of salvation as taught throughout the Bible.

THE BAPTISM OF JOHN THE BAPTIST WAS ALL THAT JESUS HAD OR THE TWELVE APOSTLES; WAS CHRISTIAN BAPTISM.

The baptism administered by John the Baptist was not distinctly Jewish, was **not** a part of ceremonial law, and did **not** belong to an Old Testament dispensation at all. In fact, the word **baptism** or **baptizing** is not even mentioned in the Old Testament. Nor is there a single reference in the Old Testament to any ceremony like the baptism of John.

It is true, as these ultra-dispensationalists point out, that the **washings** mentioned in Hebrews 9:10, **referring** to the Old Testament worship, is a translation of **baptismos,** a Greek word with the same root as **baptism,** simply a form of the same word. But the context shows that it was not the immersion of new converts who have just been saved which is referred to, but the washing or dipping of the priests' hands, and of cups and pots and brazen vessels in the big laver in connection with the bloody sacrifices of the Old Testament period. And exactly the same word in the Greek, **baptismos,** is used in Mark 7:4. There the Pharisees were complaining at Christ and the disciples because they ate with unwashen hands. Verses 3 and 4 say, "For the Pharisees, and all the Jews, except they wash their hands oft, eat not, holding the tradition of the elders. And when they come from the market, except they wash, they eat not. And many other things there be, which they have received to hold, as the washing of cups, and pots, brasen vessels, and of tables." In that passage the **washing** of Mark 7:4 is **baptismos.** When the Scripture says in that verse, "Except they wash, they eat not," the word **wash** is the very word for baptize, **baptizo.** So the only kind of baptism known in the Old Testament was the ceremonial dipping and washing of hands, or pots and cups and vessels of brass. Again I say there was nothing like John's baptism in Old Testament times. In Old Testament times there was the washing of pots and pans, ceremonial washings and dippings of the hands every day before eating. There was never, in the ceremonial law, the immersion of the whole body following repentance, picturing regeneration, a death to sin and a resurrection to new life, as New Testament baptism pictured. In the Old

Testament there is not a single case of immersion of a person as a rite similar either in form or purpose to the baptism preached and administered, according to the New Testament, by John, Jesus, and the apostles.

Anyone who says, therefore, that John's baptism was legal, or part of the ceremonial law which was for Jews only, shows that he has been getting his theology from some other book besides the Bible, and out of his ignorance misleads others who are ignorant. Again I say, baptism, in the sense that John the Baptist, Christ, and the apostles baptized, is not in the Old Testament at all. The word is not even mentioned in the Old Testament, as any one who has a good concordance can verify for himself. Baptism is entirely a New Testament doctrine and practice is connected altogether with the gospel of grace, and never with ceremonial law. In the Bible it was never administered nor commanded to any but those who publicly professed that they repented of their sins and were born again when they came in penitent faith in Christ, "the lamb of God that taketh away the sin of the world," as John preached.

It is significant that the Gospel of Mark starts out with these words, "The beginning of the gospel of Jesus Christ, the son of God; as it is written in the prophets, Behold, I send my messenger before thy face, which shall prepare thy way before thee." And then follows the story of John the Baptist and his preaching and his baptizing of converts! The gospel of Jesus Christ began with John the Baptist, says this plain Scripture! So the baptism of John the Baptist was the baptism that always should go with the gospel of Jesus Christ.

In Acts 19:1-7 is a passage which has been used by the ultra-dispensationalists to discredit John's baptism. And I am sorry to say that the Scofield Bible does the same hurtful and foolish thing. But such people "do err, not knowing the Scriptures," for the very passage itself does not reflect at all upon the baptism administered by John the Baptist and by his disciples.

Apollos had been preaching at Ephesus. The Scripture says that he was "an eloquent man, and mighty in the Scriptures" . . . "instructed in the way of the Lord; and being fervent in the spirit, he spake and taught diligently the things of the Lord, knowing only the baptism of John" (Acts 18:24, 25). That Apollos "knew only the baptism of John" does not indicate that Apollos was wrong in doctrine, for the Scriptures had already plainly said that he was "mighty in the Scriptures" and was "instructed in the way of the Lord" and that he was "fervent in the spirit" that is, that he had

the fervor of the Holy Spirit. It simply means that Apollos had been at Alexandria and elsewhere and had not been at Jerusalem when the mighty events of Pentecost transpired. Aquila and Priscilla "took him unto them, and expounded unto him the way of God more perfectly" (literally, more completely) (Acts 18:26). That is, they told him the marvelous teaching of the fulness of the Holy Spirit which Jesus had given after His resurrection, and the wonderful experiences which the disciples had had through being empowered by the Spirit. Then in Acts 18:27, 28 we are told that Apollos was greatly commended by the disciples, and that when he came to Achaia he "helped them much which had believed through grace: For he mightily convinced the Jews, and that publickly, showing by the Scriptures that Jesus was Christ."

Then comes the passage in question, Acts 19:1-7, which says,

> **"And it came to pass, that, while Apollos was at Corinth, Paul having passed through the upper coasts came to Ephesus: and finding certain disciples, He said unto them, Have ye received the Holy Ghost since ye believed? And they said unto him, We have not so much as heard whether there be any Holy Ghost. And he said unto them, Unto what then were ye baptized? And they said, Unto John's baptism. Then said Paul, John verily baptized with the baptism of repentance, saying unto the people, that they should believe on him which should come after him, that is, on Christ Jesus. When they heard this, they were baptized in the name of the Lord Jesus. And when Paul had laid his hands upon them, the Holy Ghost came on them; and they spake with tongues, and prophesied. And all the men were about twelve."**

We simply find above that Paul, coming to Ephesus, found some saved people who did not have upon them the power of the Holy Spirit which New Testament Christians had to win souls and which we ought to have.

Note that at Ephesus these men, about twelve, were "disciples" (Acts 19:1). They had "believed" (verse 2). And we know that all who have believed in Christ have everlasting life. On profession of their faith, they had been baptized (verse 3). To call such people, instructed by Apollos, unsaved, is foolish. If they were disciples who had believed and had confessed Christ openly in baptism, under the teaching of Apollos a man "mighty in the Scriptures" and "instructed in the way of the Lord" and fervent with the power of the Holy Spirit, then these people were saved. But **they did not understand that they,**

too, could have the power of the Holy Spirit! Apollos had not taught them, just as many preachers do not teach today, that Christians can have the abundant power of the Holy Spirit coming on them for soul winning.

Paul told them that they should have received this power when they were baptized. Jesus received the power of the Holy Spirit when he was baptized. And believers at Pentecost and following were taught that they should receive the power of the Holy Spirit when they were baptized (Acts 2:38). And it was expressly stated that this promise was to all that are afar off, all that God should ever call (Acts 2:39). So, these new converts at Ephesus should have had the power of the Holy Spirit upon them, too, but they did not. They had not understood fully the meaning of baptism. And so Paul baptized them again, baptizing them exactly the way that Apollos (we suppose it was Apollos) had baptized them before. Only this time they understood the sweet meaning of baptism, that the old man was dead to sin and that now they reckoned themselves dead and were raised up to live new lives in the power of the Holy Spirit. And then Paul laid his hands upon them and "the Holy Ghost came on them."

And if Paul were to come in our churches today, he could find as many as twelve men in every church of any size who do not know anything about the power of the Holy Spirit, though they may have been baptized scripturally.

I am simply saying that John's baptism was Christian baptism.

Consider that John's baptizing was all that Jesus ever had. Consider that all the disciples were baptized the same way by John the Baptist. In fact, this was the very requirement one must fulfil to be an apostle, he must be selected "of these men which have companied with us all the time that the Lord Jesus went in and out among us, Beginning from the baptism of John" said Peter in Acts 1:21,22. When Jesus was baptized by John the Baptist He said, "Thus it becometh us to fulfil all righteousness" (Matt. 3:15), and so set an example for all Christians throughout the whole age.

John's kind of baptizing is not out of date, but is to last like the gospel he preached. Wherever John's gospel that "behold the Lamb of God which taketh away the sin of the world" is preached, and wherever it is preached that "He that believeth on the Son hath everlasting life: and he that believeth not the Son shall not see life; but the wrath of God abideth on him" as John preached it (John

3:36), there new converts should be baptized the Bible way, as John the Baptist baptized them, as Jesus was baptized, as all the apostles were baptized by John, as Paul baptized his converts, and as we are commanded to baptize converts, "even unto the end of the world."

CHAPTER III.

BAPTISM FOR US IN THIS DISPENSATION; HAS NEVER BEEN DONE AWAY WITH

Sometimes when people do not want to keep some command of the Lord Jesus they say, "That was for the Jews," or "That was done away with at the closing of the apostolic age." So some people, having been accustomed to a form of baptism or a teaching about it which they could not reconcile to the Scriptures, think they can promote Christian unity by leaving off the command of Christ. Some preachers hope by leaving off baptism and letting down the bars they can attract to their churches people of all faiths. That was particularly true of a group of modernists who do not believe the Bible is authoritative and do not pretend to follow it, led by Dr. Harry Emerson Fosdick in Riverside Church, New York, and the late Dr. Shailer Mathews of the radical University of Chicago. Others call themselves fundamentalists, but hope to get away from the divisions of denominationalism by throwing away baptism. Naturally then, since they do not obey Christ's command, they try to defend themselves by quoting Scriptures. These usually teach that baptism was commanded for Jews only, or during a separate dispensation which lasted only during the age of the apostles.

That teaching, however kindly and sincere men may be who are guilty of it, is not true to the Bible. It takes away from us, for all practical use, much of the Bible, and in its effect joins with modernism and rebellion in getting people to disregard the plain commands of Christ. I believe if you will, with an open heart, study this chapter, along with the preceding one, and check the Scriptures here given with your Bible, you will see that baptism is still commanded for us, has never been done away with, and that to omit baptism is still to disobey Christ. With the exception of a few false teachers who have risen in recent years to accuse their brethren, cause divi-